UNCLUTTER!

Simple techniques
to organize your life

UNCLUTTER
your space with
FENG SHUI

Antonia Beattie and Rosemary Stevens

BARNES
&NOBLE
BOOKS
NEW YORK

Contents

Introduction:
Taking it easy — step-by-step uncluttering

HOW OFTEN HAVE YOU come home to find that there is virtually no room for you? Do you also find that you have no time for yourself and simple tasks often seem too hard to finish? The clutter in your home and the clutter in your life are connected, according to feng shui principles.

Feng shui is the ancient Chinese practice of encouraging positive energy and shielding negative energy in the home and workplace: it can have far-reaching effects on your life. According to feng shui, the flow of energy around your home affects the flow of energy around the major aspects of your life. When you clear the flow of energy in your home or workplace, you will be able to feel direct benefits in your life. Try our easy questionnaire on pages 28–29 to see when you need to take action to unclutter your home or workplace.

In this book we explore how the wise and well-proven principles of feng shui can help you unclutter your home and simplify your life. We alert you to what the clutter means in feng shui terms.

Clutter can actually hold you back. In feng shui, certain areas of your home or workplace correspond to particular areas of your life – your wealth, fame, relationships, creativity, mentors, career, education, and health (see diagram on page 15). If clutter is mainly in one area, you may find that once it is cleared, you will experience a better flow of opportunities and success in the corresponding aspect of your life.

There is much more to uncluttering than just being neat and tidy. The main concept to keep in mind is that the more material goods you throw out of your life, the more space you

create to allow positive energy to flow into your immediate surroundings and have its positive effect on your life.

You will find that when you unclutter your home and workplace you will experience better luck, and have the ability to capture those "golden opportunities" to achieve financial and personal success.

How to manage clutter? What to do with junk mail? How to cope with unwanted chipped dishes inherited from your Aunt Mimi? The most fundamental way is to set up a system of dealing with the clutter that comes through your door on a daily basis, and to clear out all the unwanted things that have gathered around you up to this point.

This book explores a number of useful and easily implemented ideas and suggestions on clearing the space around you, in order to invite a more positive form of energy into your life. We give you tips on how to make shifting the clutter from your home or workplace a higher priority. We help you get motivated, get your family members involved, and give you simple time management strategies.

Above all, this book gives you some fun ways of dealing with clutter, so that it not just another chore that you have to do every week. After being shown how to set up your own system of dealing with long-term and daily clutter, you will find that you will never experience the same buildup of clutter again. We also help you get in touch with your instincts as you make changes to your home and lifestyle.

You will find that once the clutter is gone, your life will move into new, desired directions – and you will even save money, by not buying more clutter.

The effects of clearing the clutter out of your life will be nothing short of miraculous. And clearing clutter is an enjoyable experience – for every box load of unwanted clutter you throw out or give to someone in need, you will be rewarded with more and more tangible evidence of positive energy entering your life.

Feng shui and uncluttering

The principles of the flow of qi energy

AN INVISIBLE BUT POWERFUL energy, known as chi or qi in feng shui, flows around and within you and all living things, and also around inanimate objects. Feng shui practitioners believe that this energy moves through the world like the wind ("feng"), and flows in meandering curves like water ("shui").

Qi is believed to be a combination of energies generated by the shifting balances and tensions between the earth and the cosmos. There are three interrelated types of qi – heaven qi, earth qi, and human qi.

Heaven qi is the energy of the cosmos and the movement of air above the earth. Earth qi is the energy generated by the shape of the earth, the force of its magnetic fields, and the effect of the combination of the five Chinese elements – earth, wood, fire, metal, and water. Human qi is the energy created by your personality, your thought processes, and the emotions you feel for the people around you.

In Chinese philosophy, understanding how all these aspects of energy interact and can be used is the basis of "Tao" philosophy, or "The Way."

When qi is allowed to flow in gentle curves, like a meandering river, positive energy visits all in its path. If the energy is blocked by too much clutter for example, the energy stagnates like a river that cannot flow freely because it has been blocked by debris.

There are many feng shui schools of thought. However, all feng shui practitioners agree that when qi is allowed to flow unimpeded around the house, garden or workplace, that area is lucky or auspicious. An area where there is stagnation is unlucky or inauspicious.

If the energy is permitted to run in a straight line, it tends to pick up speed and becomes like an arrow of poisonous, destructive energy. These arrows are called "sha qi" or "poison arrows," and they affect areas that are at the end of a straight line – a desk at the end of a long corridor, or a house at a "T" intersection, where the road leads straight to the building.

Poison arrows can also be generated by the angle of a corner, or a telegraph pole, or straight rooflines. They can deaden the energy of a particular room or area of your home or workplace.

You will find that if you do not block a particular area from the effect of a poison arrow, it will be virtually impossible to keep that area free from clutter. It is as if you are subconsciously using clutter to counter the effect of the poison arrow. However, there are much more elegant solutions, ones that do not also impede the flow of energy within your space, such as planting a hedge or placing a pot plant between the object generating the poison arrow and your home or cluttered area.

Clutter and the flow of positive energy

CLUTTER OF ANY FORM, whether it is a pile of magazines, an untidy desk full of paper, or a kitchen full of broken or unwashed pots, has a negative effect on the flow of energy in that area. Each area in your home or workplace corresponds to an important aspect of your life (see pages 14–15), so clutter in any area has a profound impact on the flow of positive energy in your life.

Clutter can accumulate for a number of reasons. For example, clutter can have a psychological element – you may find it difficult to let go of the past, or fear that you will not have enough support and protection in the future. It is important to remember that the more you let go of the past, the easier it is to attract new opportunities and positive energy now.

Uncluttering checklist

Check whether one or more of the following is casting poison arrows that are generating clutter in your space:

* A sharp corner on a piece of furniture
* A corner in a L-shaped room
* A corridor leading to the area
* A telegraph pole that can be seen through a window
* A sharp angle from a roofline or decoration on a neighbor's house that can be seen through a window

Try a simple experiment. Locate a cluttered area in your house, and use the checklist on the previous page to see whether a poison arrow is responsible for the clutter.

As poison arrows, by their nature, travel in straight lines, draw a straight line in your mind's eye from the object or corner generating the poison arrow to the opposite wall. Usually clutter will accumulate along the path of the poison arrow, and will be worse at the opposite wall. More often than not, clutter congregates where a poison arrow is present.

If there is no poison arrow aimed at your cluttered area, you should check whether or not there is too much space in the rest of the room. You may be making an unconscious effort to use clutter to establish a balance between yin and yang elements in a room (see pages 12–13).

Clutter also tends to accumulate in an area that relates to a particular aspiration in your life. The clutter can indicate that there is a corresponding problem within your life related to that aspiration, that an issue – and the clutter – must be cleared (see pages 14–15).

The balance between yin and yang: empty space and clutter

BALANCE IS ONE OF the most important issues in removing clutter and allowing the energy to flow through your space and your life.

Feng shui practitioners believe in finding a balance between, among other things, two universal forces – yin and yang. These forces oppose each other and are in constant motion, and the friction between them creates the flow of positive energy through the various levels of life and the cosmos.

Yin corresponds with female, passive energy, dark colors and the space within an interior. Yang corresponds with male, aggressive energy, light colors and the furniture and objects in your space.

Consequently, clutter is closely related to yang energy. Too much yang energy in a space will make you feel tired and listless, as if the energy around you has been stimulated to breaking point.

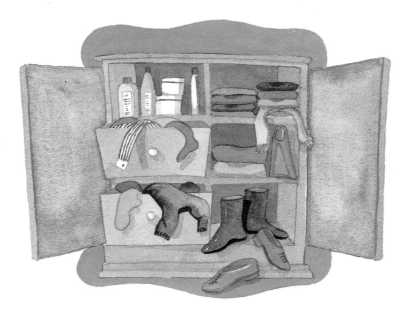

Uncluttering checklist

Walk into a cluttered room or area and analyze whether there is an imbalance in the yin and yang energies in the room. You will find "yin space" rooms and areas tend to attract clutter more than other rooms. "Yin space" rooms often have the following characteristics:

✴ The color of the walls or carpet is dark, cool, gray–green or blue
✴ The area or room is overly large or overly small
✴ The area or room is poorly lit
✴ The area is near water pipes where stagnation and leaking can occur

If a workplace is cluttered, a manager should not be surprised that employees miss their deadlines or are unable to finish their jobs in time. At home, too much yang energy can lead to arguments that seem to have no resolution.

Balancing yin and yang is the key to knowing how much stuff to get rid of. If a room is too large, clutter will tend to accumulate as an unconscious attempt to balance the "yin space" with "yang objects."

The reason we try to achieve this balance is that we instinctively know that once yin and yang are balanced, the life force around us will also be balanced. We then usually experience prosperity, good health and luck in our lives.

"Yin space" rooms and areas include bedrooms, kitchen and bathroom cupboards, and large areas such as lofts, oversized family rooms and open-plan areas.

There are many ways of counterbalancing the clutter that accumulates in these areas. If you need to clear clutter in cupboards, try putting in more shelving or installing a light, especially if it can be set up so that the light only turns on when you open the door to the cupboard. In oversized rooms, you can relieve your clutter problems by slowly acquiring storage furniture – the yang energy of these pieces will also help balance the "yin space" of the room.

Why should we unclutter?

What is your house trying to tell you?

THE FACT THAT CERTAIN areas of your home or workplace always seem to attract clutter can indicate a corresponding problem in your life. As the clutter grows, so does your problem. If the clutter is cleared, your problem will also be cleared. This concept in feng shui stems from the idea that all forms of energy are related – if you change the energy on one level, there will be corresponding changes on other levels.

In feng shui, there are eight important aspirations of life. These eight aspirations correspond to compass directions:

ASPIRATION	COMPASS DIRECTION	ASPIRATION	COMPASS DIRECTION
Wealth	Southeast	Children, creativity	West
Fame	South	Education	Northeast
Relationships	Southwest	Career	North
Family and health	East	Mentors, travel	Northwest

To use the grid so that you can find out where the clutter is indicating problems in your life, draw a floor plan of your home or workplace on a piece of tracing paper. On a separate piece of paper, draw an octagon or bagua (an eight-sided shape, like the one on the next page) big enough to cover the whole floor plan of your space. Subdivide and label the octagon as

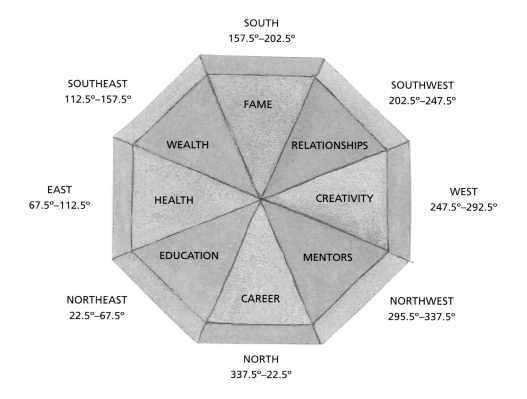

SOUTH
157.5°–202.5°

SOUTHEAST
112.5°–157.5°

SOUTHWEST
202.5°–247.5°

FAME

WEALTH

RELATIONSHIPS

EAST
67.5°–112.5°

HEALTH

CREATIVITY

WEST
247.5°–292.5°

EDUCATION

MENTORS

NORTHEAST
22.5°–67.5°

CAREER

NORTHWEST
295.5°–337.5°

NORTH
337.5°–22.5°

shown above. Stand at your front door or entry to your space and, with your back to the door, hold a compass in your hand and find out approximately what direction your door is facing.

Place the bagua under the floor plan, matching the direction that your door is facing with the correct side of the bagua. Align that side of the bagua with your door, making sure that the bagua covers the whole floor plan. Trace the internal lines of the bagua onto your floor. This will give you a general indication of where the aspirations fall in your space. Now walk through your space and mark onto your floor plan where the clutter is accumulating. If you clear the clutter from these areas, you will feel a marked improvement in the area of life that the clutter was stifling. If you find that the clutter keeps coming back, hang a natural crystal over the clutter and follow the other suggestions in this book. Natural crystal has a powerful ability to disperse negative energy, giving you a chance to clear the clutter so that it won't come back.

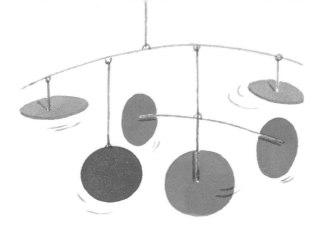

Clearing the energy before clearing the clutter

HUMAN-MADE OBJECTS, SUCH AS buildings, the decorations we use inside them, and the over-accumulation of household or work-related objects, can disrupt the flow of qi. Once the flow is disrupted, it can become a dangerous force that has far-reaching effects on our lives.

If the energy is slowed down, it can stagnate, causing a room or part of a room to feel muted and become cluttered. This will have a corresponding effect in your life, and you will find it very hard to make shifts or find new opportunities in your life because you cannot see through the confusion of your circumstances. If the qi is made to travel too fast, it becomes a poison arrow, which can cause arguments, breakages and other disruptions in your life wherever its aggressive energy hits. Clutter can also accumulate in these areas to form a barricade against the hostile energy of a poison arrow.

Even if clutter is used successfully as a shield, it slows down the positive energy as well as the negative. So clutter is never a good way to rebalance the flow of energy through your space. Clutter is a symptom, and it requires a cure – a feng shui cure.

The first step is to remove or screen off any destructive energy. Do this before you start putting objects back in their right place or throwing junk out of the space. The second step is to place a feng shui cure near the clutter to rebalance the flow of energy in a particular area.

The following table lists a number of common feng shui cures and gives suggestions on when to use them and in what area of your space (in terms of compass directions). Refer to the floor plan that you made (see pages 14–15) to check which aspiration corresponds to each compass direction.

FENG SHUI CURE	WHEN TO USE THE CURE	BEST AREA TO USE THE CURE (compass direction)
Color	Use bright, yang colors such as red, orange, and yellow to stimulate the stagnant, cluttered energy in a dark area or cupboard	West
Lights, mirrors, and crystals	Use these cures to deflect a poison arrow	South
Metal chimes and bells	Use these cures to activate stagnant energy – hang over the clutter	Northwest
Mobiles and flags	Use these cures to attract positive energy – hang over the clutter	Southwest
Statues and rocks	Use to slow down energy traveling in a straight line – place in a long corridor or path leading to the cluttered area	West
Fans and flutes	Use to deflect a poison arrow	East
Music	Use to stimulate stagnant energy	Northeast

Twelve good reasons to
unclutter your home and office

GOOD REASONS ABOUND to unclutter your space. The more objects you accumulate, the more you become bogged down with maintaining the clutter you have. If you calculate the time and money you spend on storing, removing, cleaning, and organizing your treasures, you may be surprised to see how little time you have left for the things you actually want to do.

It is not only your time that may be lost. Robbery and theft are serious concerns for many householders. Thieves, attracted by the saleable commodities in your home or office space, need to be dissuaded from robbing your premises – many people use security systems, and have people mind their houses while they are away.

Clutter not only stops the flow of beneficial energy, it also stops you from moving as freely as you would like to. Freeing yourself from the binds of unnecessary clutter can help you focus on yourself and your family, sending your family and friends the message that you and they are much more important than possessions.

Here are twelve very good reasons to unclutter your home and workspace.

REASON 1	You will feel empowered by your ability to control your space, rather than being controlled by the space.
REASON 2	Uncluttering will help you move through life more effortlessly.
REASON 3	Through uncluttering, you will feel lighter and find it easier to reach your desired goals quickly.
REASON 4	Clearing clutter will let new opportunities and possibilities become more evident.
REASON 5	Having a mindset that will not allow clutter to accumulate means that you will limit spending on unnecessary things and will eventually save money.
REASON 6	Uncluttering will give you extra space in which to live and work.
REASON 7	Once you have uncluttered, you will feel more comfortable about inviting family and friends into your space – you won't have to hide the clutter and go into a panic-driven frenzy of cleaning.
REASON 8	You will enjoy being able to open a cupboard door without having things fall on you.
REASON 9	You will feel balanced and in tune by having a place for everything, and everything in its place.
REASON 10	Uncluttering will help you find items quickly and easily.
REASON 11	Uncluttering will help you create a more harmonious environment.
REASON 12	Uncluttering will give you the opportunity to give things to people less fortunate than you.

The ultimate benefits
of uncluttering

CLUTTER IS A SYMBOL of being held back. There may be important reasons for seeking protection from going forward in your life. However, sometimes when the reason for holding yourself back is no longer valid, you are still stuck with old decisions and old motivations.

If you suspect that you have stuff around you that is no longer a reflection of who you really are now, clear the air and let new energy into your life by uncluttering your space.

You will be astonished at the myriad positive effects that will emerge. First and foremost, you will attract a better flow of energy in your house and in your life. You will also notice a marked improvement in luck and prosperity for all the people who share the house with you.

The aim of uncluttering your space is to put every area of your life into perspective and balance. You will then be able to see clearly what you want, and you will have more time to do what you want.

If you feel that you just don't know which path to follow in your life, clear the clutter from your home and you will find, even as you are clearing the junk out, that ideas and thoughts of new directions come to you.

You will also find that the skills you gain as you clear the accumulated clutter of the past will help you keep your life simple and organized. You will be able to find things much more quickly. You will also find that you can manage the flow of daily clutter easily, and that your workload will seem less overwhelming.

Once being organized becomes second nature to you, you will see more opportunities for advancement and will be in an excellent position to capitalize on them. This is an especially important skill for those who are contemplating working from home. Eventually, you will find that the day-to-day running of your household and business will be almost no drain on your energy.

Another positive aspect of uncluttering your space is the financial savings you will make. Remember that any new item depreciates in value as soon as you walk out of the retailer's door. Why not redirect that money to investments or to experiences that directly nurture your soul?

When you unclutter, you will find that you have more funds available to cover those major expenses and bills, as well as spare money to spend on your dream holiday, a soothing massage or a nurturing beauty treatment.

Getting clutter out of your life

Managing long-term clutter

FOUR OF THE MOST important questions to ask yourself when faced with the prospect of clearing long-term clutter from your space are:

* Am I going to use this item?
* What is this item for?
* Is this item a "want" or a "need?"
* Will I be seriously inconvenienced if I throw this item away?

Storing an object that you will use in the future is valid. However, you must be able to identify when in the future will you use the item, and how often. If any question mark about its use lingers, it is best to get rid of it.

If you have hardware items (such as a power saw), remember that you are responsible for keeping them in good condition. You must be able to store them properly so that they don't get damaged and will stay in good working order.

Storage of other items, such as nails or paint, must also be carefully planned – nails will rust if they are incorrectly stored, and paint will crust over and become unusable.

Remember, if you choose to store something, you are responsible for its proper maintenance. It's important that your belongings' future use will not be undermined by poor maintenance and storage, and that they will not quickly become useless pieces of junk.

Also make sure that you know for what purpose an item will be used. If you don't know what it is, get rid of it. How many of us have leads with differently shaped plugs that have been gathering dust for years in a cupboard somewhere?

Also ask yourself whether you actually need the item or whether you only want it. If you are definitely going to use the object, then you need it and must find a suitable place to store it and look after it. If you just simply like the look of the object, or it was on sale and you couldn't resist buying it, then you wanted to acquire the object to fulfill an emotional need. However, buying an object is often not enough to actually quench your need to show how clever you were to find something that is both beautiful and cheap, or to remind you of a time or place when you were much happier.

That is not to say that you should not buy decorative objects at all. If you are buying a decorative item, make sure that it fits into your lifestyle and interior design, and that it is of good quality. William Morris, a famous craftsperson of the nineteenth century, believed that a person should only own things that are useful or beautiful.

Clutter location checklist

CLUTTER CAN BUILD UP in a number of key areas. Go to each of the places identified in the checklist on the next page and answer the questions before taking action to clear the clutter. The checklist is designed to help you clear the clutter, and then keep the clutter away permanently.

Take a pen and a copy of the checklist below as you go around your home or workplace and answer the two questions. The first question tries to identify where clutter has accumulated. The clutter will usually give you a sense of stagnation – you may feel that the air in this space is not fresh or clean. The second question is designed to help you notice any features that have created poison arrows aimed at the area in question; if there are, they may be the reason why the clutter has built up over time.

LOCATION	QUESTION 1 Is there a lot of clutter in this area?	QUESTION 2 Is there a poison arrow aimed at this location?
Entrance to the home		
Hall table		
Bookcases		
Coffee table		
Kitchen table		
Kitchen bench tops		
Kitchen cupboards		
Kitchen drawers		
Bedroom floors		
Bedroom closets		
Storage space in the cellar		
Storage space under the stairs		
Linen cabinet		
Cupboards		
Storage space in the attic		
Garage		
Your car		
Garden shed		
Garden		
Study or computer room		
Filing cabinet		
Desk or workbench top		
Desk drawers		
Hidden areas at your place or work		
Workplace storage cupboards or bookshelves		
Outside storage facilities		
Storage at the homes of your friends or relatives		

Setting up the basics

WHEN YOU ARE READY to start the uncluttering process, you will need to set up a temporary area inside or outside your home or workplace. This is the area where you can immediately place the trash and unwanted objects, until you are ready to take it to the dump, to a charitable organization or to give it to someone who wants it.

Setting up this area allows you to get the trash out of your selected space immediately. You may decide to have a temporary uncluttering storage area in the garage, in a prefabricated work shed bought specially for the job, or in the health area, or in the areas of your space that correspond with the health or family aspirations (see pages 14–15).

This area should be kept tidy and clean while you sort through and work out what to do with your clutter. If you do not keep this uncluttering space well organized, you may precipitate health problems for yourself.

To organize your temporary uncluttering storage area, consider setting up several large bins or bags for different types of clutter. Have bins or bags set up for each of the following categories:

* Keeping but needs to go in another area
* Unsure about throwing away
* Recycling (giving to another person or charitable organization)
* Recycling trash (recyclable trash, such as cans, bottles, and newspapers)
* Throwing away outright.

Those objects in the area that you are currently uncluttering that you have chosen to keep can simply be left where they are. Clean them with a damp cloth or polish their surface, and clean each surface that you have uncluttered.

If you have a pair of Tibetan bells or a melodic-sounding hand bell, ring the bell over the surface you have uncluttered. At the end of a day's worth of uncluttering or a discrete period of uncluttering, ring the Tibetan bells or hand bell over the temporary uncluttering storage area to help keep the energy flowing through that space, too.

Place a mirror on the door or entrance leading to the temporary uncluttering storage area. In feng shui, the mirror creates an illusion that the room does not exist.

So that you do not leave the clutter in your temporary setup, hang wind chimes or a natural crystal over the bins or bags. At the end of the day, go through your "unsure" pile and ask yourself the following questions (see pages 22–23):

* Am I going to use this item?
* What is this item for?
* Is this item a "want" or a "need?"
* Will I be seriously inconvenienced if I throw this item away?

If you still feel doubtful about whether or not you should discard the item, just bite the bullet and throw or give it away. That you are doubtful is a sure sign that you don't really need the object.

Knowing when to take action:
an in-depth questionnaire

ANSWER THE FOLLOWING QUESTIONNAIRE to assess your need for uncluttering your space:

	QUESTION	YES	NO
1	Do you drive a station wagon or a pick-up so that you can pick up items from the side of the road?		
2	Do you have roof racks on your car, as well as ropes and spare blankets in the trunk so that you can carry things home without paying for delivery?		
3	Do you feel compelled to stop and rummage when you see junk piled on the side of the road?		
4	Do you feel compelled to buy things that have been marked down in price?		
5	Do you usually buy damaged goods or factory seconds?		
6	Do you prefer to buy wholesale?		
7	Does glossy advertising for "specials" get you excited?		
8	Do you often go to the shops or the mall when you are feeling down?		
9	Would you prefer to buy rather than hire machinery that you probably will not use again?		
10	If someone wants to start a new hobby, do you have all the equipment to help them get started?		
11	Have you lost something two years ago and still not found it?		
12	Are your family members embarrassed by the amount of stuff you have in the house?		
13	Have your children stopped asking their friends home?		

	QUESTION	YES	NO
14	Do you allow other people to store their stuff with you?		
15	Do you still have boxed gifts that are unopened because they are too good to use?		
16	Has a friend or relative given you things that you really don't want or cannot use?		
17	Have you got clothes in your wardrobe that are of different sizes?		
18	Have you got shoes that have been worn through?		
19	Do you find that there are certain rooms you do not go into because there is too much stuff in them?		
20	Do you have certain cupboards that you do not open because the items will fall out?		

If you have answered yes to any of the questions, you need to consider uncluttering your space. If you were given a fire extinguisher as a gift by a friend or family member who was concerned that you would go up in smoke quickly because of all the junk in your home or workspace, unclutter your space immediately!

Identifying clutter

Various grades of clutter

CLUTTER COMES IN MANY shapes and forms, and can accumulate for a variety of reasons. Clutter can fall into the following categories:

- ✴ Objects that are still useful but are simply kept in the wrong place, such as cookbooks stored in a bedroom bookcase
- ✴ Objects that are still useful but need professional repair, such as a video recorder
- ✴ Objects that are beyond repair, such as an old washing machine for which the parts are no longer available
- ✴ Parts of objects that once broken, have never been reassembled, such as a once-treasured toy
- ✴ Old newspapers, newsletters and magazines
- ✴ Other kinds of paper, such as old receipts that are no longer needed for taxation purposes
- ✴ Packaging, plastic bags, rusty metal, torn clothes, moldy shoes.

You will probably have items in a number of the above categories that fall under the heading of junk. To help you decide what is junk, turn to pages 32–33. However, you may also have some items that could be classified as memorabilia, and each of these must be carefully considered (see pages 34–35).

When you are sorting out the clutter that surrounds you, keep in mind that some of the things you have do still serve a purpose – they are just not in the right area of your home or office to be of use to you. For instance, you may have a wonderful collection of cookbooks, but if they are not near at hand when you are planning your grocery shopping or working out a meal plan, you might as well have no cookbooks at all. Watch what you do in the day and make sure that the things that you have around you are the things you need to do your daily tasks.

Feng shui uncluttering anecdote

Paul, a successful plumber, was asked by a friend to fix a dishwasher. Paul had a look at it and, after dismantling it, found that the dishwasher just could not be repaired. He then left the broken machine sitting beside the front door to his business. The broken dishwasher stayed there for quite a while. Soon Paul found that his business had slowed down, for no perceivable reason – he had always had a steady and reliable clientele – and that he was owed money. When his friend rang to find out how the repairs were coming along, Paul finally asked him to take the machine away. With the machine gone, Paul was delighted to find that virtually the next day the money that was owed to him came in the mail and his business grew back to where it had been before the dishwasher arrived on his premises.

What is junk?

JUNK IS THE WORST kind of clutter. It slows down the flow of qi in the house to such an extent that the room in which the junk resides will feel stagnant and unwelcoming. It can be any one of the following:

* Items that are broken and unusable
* Objects you have never liked
* Decorative objects that do not suit your interior design
* Decorative or useful objects that do not suit your lifestyle
* Objects that remind you of an unhappy time in your life or evoke unresolved feelings
* Objects that do not serve your life purpose
* Objects that require a lot of cleaning and are generally high maintenance
* Objects that never get used and are always just stored
* Objects that are more trouble than they are worth
* Clothes that don't fit anymore
* Shoes that are beyond repair.

Feng shui uncluttering tip

When you go shopping, ask for less packaging or take a shopping bag with you. You may wish to hang two small drawstring bags from your kitchen pantry door or some other convenient place, and put your reusable plastic bags into them. Use one drawstring bag for large plastic bags and the other for smaller ones.

Apart from asking the usual four uncluttering questions (see pages 22–23), also ask yourself: "Who am I storing this for?" Storing clutter can be a symptom of feeling insecure about the future. Sometimes the answer to "Who am I storing this for?" may actually be "a future me" or "my children." Turn to pages 36–37 for some simple ways of dealing with the fear of letting go of the clutter with which you have surrounded yourself.

Feng shui uncluttering anecdote

Annette organized a divorce party with a difference. She had collected all the items from her marriage – photos, sentimental items and furniture – and asked her guests to take whatever they liked. Items left over were consigned to a bonfire to clear the energy of the unhappy marriage from Annette's life. After the party, Annette felt as if an enormous load had been taken off her shoulders.

What are memorabilia?

MEMORABILIA, COLLECTIBLES AND ANTIQUES require special consideration in the uncluttering process. You must weigh up whether these items are holding you back and keeping you in the past or evoking cherished memories that help you feel connected to your family and loved ones.

What are memorabilia? Memorabilia are items that you have collected or that have been passed down to you that have a special meaning to you or your family. These items can include recipe books from your grandmother, woodwork tools from your grandfather, or a handmade quilt from your favorite aunt.

However, these items require special care. For instance, your grandmother's cookbook may be falling to pieces or the quilt may need cleaning. Consider copying your favorite recipes from the book and storing the book in a safe place out of your kitchen, maybe even

Feng shui uncluttering tip

In feng shui, the wisdom of the ancestors of the family is specially venerated. Consider storing a small selection of memorabilia in the family and health area of your home (see pages 14–15). You may wish to make a cheerful arrangement in that area. Hang some images of butterflies in the area – they are feng shui symbols of joy and harmony.

out of your house (you may store it in your home if you have enough space and the flow of qi is not disturbed).

You may also consider passing items of memorabilia on to other members of the family who have expressed an interest in them. Passing these items along to the family or your group of special friends will have a positive effect on the flow of energy around the object, avoiding stagnation and keeping the memory of a loved one alive.

Memorabilia can also include collectibles and antiques. You may have inherited some furniture or porcelain through your family or have collected objects, such as baseball cards or certain toys. These may be quite valuable.

However, you will only get a good price for these items if they have been properly stored and looked after. For instance, the baseball cards may need to be stored in acid-free boxes or wrapped in acid-free paper, and the boxes the toys came in must be kept, so that the toys stay in mint condition.

If you are prepared to do this, by all means keep the items and watch their price gradually grow. If you are not prepared to go to such trouble, find a reputable dealer or auction house and get your pieces properly valued and disposed of.

Dealing with the fear of letting go: what to do if you just can't let go

YOU MAY FIND THAT the whole concept of uncluttering your space is just too daunting. If you do, do not despair. Uncluttering doesn't have to be an arduous chore. You can unclutter in small chunks, working on one small group of your possessions at a time, such as your accessories or the sock drawer (see pages 50–51).

If you have difficulty discarding some items, consider packing them in a box and placing them neatly in a storage area. Make a note in your diary or special "Uncluttering Journal" (see pages 62–63) to check in 12 months whether you have needed the things in the box. If you haven't missed them for 12 months, it is time to let them go.

Clutter may be an indication of a problem within a particular feng shui aspiration in your life. Work out where the clutter congregates and what that means in feng shui to your life (see pages 14–15). This will give you motivation to unclutter your space, particularly when you start seeing an improvement in that particular aspiration.

Clutter may also be an indication that you fear to let go of the possessions around you. There can be a number of reasons for this. For instance, the clutter may represent a form of protection that you are using as your armor. Answer the following questions to check whether the need for this form of added protection is valid. If you answer "yes" to any one of the questions on the next page, we give you alternative, more efficient forms of protection.

Feng shui uncluttering checklist

* Can you see a poison arrow aimed at the area that is accumulating clutter (see pages 10–11)?
  If you can, consider blocking the feature creating the poison arrow by using a mirror, plant, crystal, or wind chime.

* Are you living or working in a safe neighborhood?
  If you are not, consider installing an effective security system.

* Do you feel emotionally vulnerable?
  If you do, consider talking about your feelings to a friend or a counselor. Uncluttering will help you clear old patterns of behavior and look at problems and difficult issues in a different way.

If you are finding it difficult to discard things, you could ask a good friend, one who will not give in to your excuses, to help you. If you are finding that the clutter keeps coming back, you may also wish to consult a clutter professional (see pages 52–53).

Uncluttering and storage solutions

Where to store and how to discard

STORE THINGS YOU KNOW you will not need immediately but will need within the next 12 months. Keep these items to a minimum and avoid storing them under furniture, especially your bed.

In feng shui, it is considered very inauspicious to store any clutter or unused things under the bed – if these things are under the bed, the person using the bed will experience restless sleep and insomnia, through trying to sleep on top of stagnant energy.

Feng shui uncluttering anecdote

Shirley, a mother of a lovely daughter, had great difficulty deciding whether to have another child. She stored her daughter's baby clothes under the bed and was consequently sleeping directly above her difficult decision, which was made even harder by the stagnation of energy under her bed. Within two weeks of being advised to store the baby clothes in a box in her garage, Shirley came to a final decision not to have more children. Once she had made the decision, Shirley was able to let go of the baby's clothes – she sent them to a family friend who was expecting a child.

Storing clothes and objects in the basement can also cause stagnation of energy. Cluttering your basement with junk is akin to storing clutter under your bed, but on a larger scale. All aspects of your life will feel stagnant and you will feel that you are going nowhere.

Similarly, storing or dumping clutter in the attic can have a negative effect on your life. The unresolved issues that some of these items represent will feel overbearing and intrusive. You may find that you suffer from headaches, even migraines. Keep both the attic and the basement clear of clutter, and store only things you will use within a reasonable period of time – we suggest 12 months.

If you have already worked out what to throw out, it is important that you dispose of your clutter in a responsible way. First, find out how much of your clutter you can recycle. For instance, can the paper or newspapers be recycled? If your paperwork is fairly sensitive material, consider shredding it and sending it to a pet store. Pet stores are often happy to receive shredded paper to line the cages for their animals.

Second, you may be able to recycle the objects or garments by giving them to a friend or a charitable organization. Perhaps you could have an uncluttering party, where everyone who comes can take their pick of your clutter.

Useful storage ideas

STORAGE IN YOUR LIVING and working areas must either be out of sight or well arranged. The storage room, garage, or off-site location, must be arranged so that you can move freely in it and access each box or item easily. If you have full boxes left over that won't fit into your storage space, you need to reassess what you are storing. This is an unavoidable message, telling you that you do not have enough space around you or in your life to deal with this excess.

In feng shui, objects have yang energy. To counterbalance the high levels of yang energy created by the boxes of stuff in your storage area, consider covering the boxes with yin-colored fabric or packing your objects into dark-colored boxes. Yin colors include blues, greens, blacks and dark browns. And remember, don't pack your boxes tightly. Leave room within each box for qi energy to circulate.

In feng shui, the world is made up of five elements – earth, metal, water, wood, and fire. Add objects that correspond with the element of wood, such as wooden shelves, to help stabilize the energy in your storage area, as boxes and papers relate to the wood element. As metal is destructive to wood (think of an axe chopping down a tree), using metal shelves will create an underlying current of tension in your storage space.

In feng shui, balance is important in the interior of your environment because the balance in your furniture, objects and storage spaces allows qi to circulate harmoniously in your space.

You can create balance simply by maintaining an even number of objects on show, or an even number of whatever storage systems you have chosen. For instance, place two, four, or six candles on display in a particular area. To bring more harmony to your space, consider placing objects that correspond to one of the five elements on display in an area that corresponds to a particular compass direction (see the table above).

TYPE OF STORAGE OBJECTS	CORRESPONDING ELEMENT	CORRESPONDING COMPASS DIRECTION OR POSITION IN THE ROOM
Ceramics	Earth	Near the center of the room
Jewelry, metal frames, and bowls	Metal	West
Wicker items, paper products	Wood	East
Cups, glasses, and decanters	Water	North
Candles and incense	Fire	South

Keep an eye out for decorative storage items that have potential as containers for some of those trivial but useful pieces of equipment or other items that otherwise tend to be found all over the place. By keeping such things as rubber bands, paper clips, and small useful hardware items in one place, you will save time – more time than you realize.

Use your imagination regarding how you would like to store some of these smaller objects. Keep an eye out for useful or unusual boxes or baskets, such as a decoupage wastepaper basket that is big enough to store all your socks, a decoratively woven basket for your towels, or a metal cookie tin for all your needles and thread.

Using off-site storage

OFF-SITE STORAGE IS USEFUL for objects that you do not often need or documents that you have to keep to comply with the legal and operational requirements of your business or industry.

The same rules apply to off-site storage as to storage in your house, garage, or workplace. Make sure that you are able to easily access the storage area, that everything is stacked neatly, and that all boxes or items are also easy to access. Don't pack the boxes tightly. Leave room within the box for the qi energy to circulate.

It is important that your storage area – on-site or off-site – is not used as a dumping ground. If the things you want to store do not fit into your storage area, consider reducing the number of items you are hoping to store. Ask yourself the four essential uncluttering questions (see pages 22–23).

Offices often need solutions to storage problems too – office managers may need to consider using professional businesses that can offer a secure storage solution for paper and electronic materials. However, a number of issues need to be looked into before a storage company is chosen.

First, evaluate the level of security you need and whether the off-site storage company can provide that level of security. Second, you will also need to evaluate the position of the

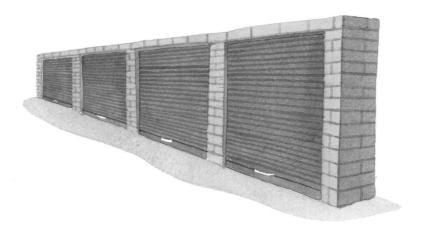

storage area – is it safe from earthquake, flood or power failure? Third, if you are storing items or paper, you should also find out whether the storage facility is climate controlled.

Another feng shui recommendation is to check that the doors to the storage facility do not stick and that you have access to your stored items when you need it.

When you pack the items you are going to store off-site, do it slowly and thoroughly, and make sure you itemize what is being stored and set up a system so that you know where to find each item.

It is always a good idea to include, preferably stuck on the inside of each box lid, a description of what is stored in that box. Have a corresponding list in a file that can be easily accessed in your home or workplace, or stick the list into your "Uncluttering Journal" (see pages 62–63).

Getting started

Simple strategies to clear clutter:
everyone together

USUALLY IT ONLY NEEDS one person to motivate a whole family or workplace to get serious about clearing clutter. As you are the one reading this book, you will most probably be the one to set the uncluttering process in motion. If you need to know how to keep yourself and your colleagues or family motivated, see pages 46–47.

Here is a simple six-step plan you can follow to help you set up an uncluttering framework at home or at work. Once the framework is set up, you will find that family members and work colleagues find it hard to resist.

STEP 1	Make a floor plan as suggested on pages 14–15, then work out where the eight aspirations of life fall on the plan.
STEP 2	Take a simple stroll around your home or office, marking down on the floor plan the various areas in which clutter has accumulated.
STEP 3	See if you can locate any especially obvious objects or long straight corridors within and outside your space where "poison arrows" are being created, causing clutter to accumulate (see pages 16–17). Note on your plan where the poison arrows are being generated and which areas they are hitting.
STEP 4	Do a guesstimate of how much stuff needs to be thrown away, recycled, stored, moved to another, more functional area, or simply left where it is.
STEP 5	Select an appropriate place for organizing the clutter and adopt the setting-up-the-basics strategies outlined on pages 26–27.
STEP 6	Select an appropriate place for storing all the items you will need to use in the next 12 months (see pages 38–43).

Do not be afraid to be a leader in the uncluttering process. Using this six-step plan will help arm you with the information you need to convince others that there is an advantage in clearing the clutter from your shared space.

In particular, doing steps 1 and 2 (above), will help you show that some of the problems and issues you and your family or work colleagues are experiencing may be caused by the stagnation of energy in a particular aspiration. For instance, poor profits in a business can be turned around by clearing the clutter from the wealth area of the workplace, and from the wealth area of the owner's (or owners') home.

Once armed with this data, call an information-gathering meeting of your family or work colleagues. Set a time and an agenda for your first meeting and begin a dialogue so that you and the other participants can air your feelings and ideas about the clutter in the home or workplace. Lead the meeting, and show everyone your findings, and what can be done to set up the uncluttering process.

Getting motivated

KEEPING YOURSELF AND YOUR family, work colleagues or management motivated about uncluttering may be difficult, but there are a number of ideas that will help you stave off lethargy and keep the interest going.

Once the uncluttering process has been set up (see pages 44–45), have another meeting with your family or work colleagues to share any experiences encountered while working on clearing long-term clutter. This will help everyone feel that they are pulling together as a team on the project.

At the meeting, you may wish to canvas how you can all keep one other motivated to do something about the clutter. Try out some of the following suggestions at the meeting:

* We should not purchase anything except necessities until the clutter is either organized or disposed of
* We should set a limit on our spending for certain items
* We should aim to have some money left in our budget at the end of a specified period. (You may wish to discuss what the spare money could be used for. For instance, you may all decide to set the money aside for a charitable or other specific purpose.)
* We should set up a chart and have a system in which each specified uncluttering project completed by a person or a team will earn a gold star, and a certain number of gold stars will earn a particular prize, such as a weekend away.

For motivation, read pages 14–21, about why you should unclutter your space. Keep in mind that clearing clutter has important ramifications for your business, family, and health.

In terms of your business, clearing clutter will give you focus, as well as a sense of direction for your life's work or for how to make your business thrive. Clutter stagnates the energy around you and your activities, so clearing it will stop you feeling stuck.

In terms of your family, when you clear the clutter you will find that arguments over where things are, where they should be and who used them last will cease. Over time, you will experience the more harmonious flow of energy in family relationships that an ordered household can bring.

In terms of health, if you have been ill, the uncluttering process may help you locate the products or materials that have made you unwell. Asthma and allergy sufferers will particularly benefit from a cleaner and fresher home. Clearing clutter will also increase your level of vitality, as you will no longer be weighed down by the sight of disorder and consequent feelings of frustration.

If the clutter in your home or office is overwhelming, it may be a good idea to hold your uncluttering meetings away from the cluttered space. Choose a comfortable yet uncluttered environment, maybe a friend's place or business premises, to inspire and help motivate your family or staff.

Setting up a workable agenda

ONCE YOU AND YOUR family or work colleagues feel motivated to tackle the clutter around you, you should set up a workable agenda for the uncluttering process. This agenda should make it very clear what the uncluttering tasks are and who should do which task. Remember, everyone takes his or her own time to decide what is important, so first make a date to meet and establish guidelines.

Several questions need to be asked before an agenda can be set, including the following:

* What do we already have in our home that can be used to help us organize our life or business?
* What do we need to purchase to help us manage our personal or desktop items?

Do you need more storage units or containers? It is wise to have a good look at the clutter and make a note in a notebook or your "Uncluttering Journal" (see pages 62–63) of what kind of containers or storage system will suit what you have. Otherwise, you may end up trying to fit your things into a storage system you already have rather than tailoring a storage system to suit you. Take your time to find the right storage system for the objects you need for your home or business, even if you purchase just one box or container at a time. In the meantime, reuse some of the empty boxes that were saved for a rainy day or that were storing useless items or trash.

Make sure your agenda includes time to do the following things (use the list on the next page as a template, tailoring it to suit your own circumstances) once the uncluttering process has been set up (see pages 44–45).

When you have finished uncluttering a certain spot, such as a drawer or cupboard, ring a bell in each corner to remove the last vestige of stagnant energy from it. When you have finished an entire area, light a candle and a stick of incense or a sage smudge stick and feel the positive energy of qi returning to the space.

ACTIVITY	LIST	DUE DATE
Identify the main areas that need uncluttering	For example: Bathroom　　　Laundry　　　Kitchen Coffee table　　Downstairs cupboard Basement　　　Attic	
Identify who wants to be responsible for each area	For example: Kitchen – Mary　　　　Bathroom – Greg Laundry – Steven　　　Coffee table – Anna Attic – Steven　　　　Basement – Greg Downstairs cupboard – Anna	
Identify what tasks need to be done in each area	For example: Kitchen – cutlery drawer　　　– utensils drawer – fridge　　　　　　　– glasses cupboard – pots and pans　　　– fresh foodstuffs – canned foodstuffs　– packet food – pantry cupboard	
Within each task, identify and throw away certain clutter		
Within each task, identify and recycle certain clutter		
Within each task, identify and move some items to another area		
Within each task, identify and move certain items for storage		
Within each task, identify and double check what should be left where it is		

Simple time-management ideas

WHEN CONTEMPLATING REMOVING LONG-TERM clutter, remember that it will take a while for you to clear your space. After all, it may have taken you a lifetime to accumulate the clutter!

It is probably unreasonable to expect to clear all your clutter in one day, unless you really wish to make a fresh start, leaving everything behind. This approach can have advantages, but it will not give you the insight into your life that consciously and carefully uncluttering your space can give you.

By uncluttering slowly and using the agenda suggested on pages 48–49, you will give yourself enough time to thoroughly contemplate each important item and make the right decision about whether you are going to keep it or throw it away.

Making your uncluttering jobs small – do-able in an evening or in even smaller time periods, such as fifteen minutes or half an hour – will help simplify your life, and can even become fun.

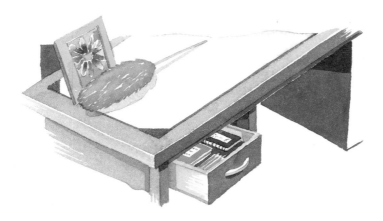

A step-by-step approach to uncluttering can help you get in touch with your past and may help you resolve issues that you have not had the time or the energy to examine. The process can also help you get in touch with your likes and dislikes. Uncluttering can help you free yourself from items that others have wanted you to have and expectations that have been placed on you by others.

However, it is important to keep an agenda or list of what needs to be uncluttered so that you do not fall behind in your plan to unclutter your home or workplace. Give yourself deadlines so that you can finish one task on your list or agenda per day or per week.

If you are doing your uncluttering once a week, make it the same day and time each week, so that you develop a routine of uncluttering. Similarly, if you are doing your uncluttering daily, choose the same time slot each day. By choosing the same time or day, you are training your mind to incorporate this activity into your daily routine, which may also stabilize the rest of your existing routine.

If your uncluttering task does not take up the full half-hour, do not start on another task. Leave it for the next day or the next week. It is important not to discourage yourself by attempting to tackle too big a job.

When choosing the time for daily uncluttering, select a time when you are still active from the day. For example, if you walk the dog straight after work, slot in a half-hour uncluttering session between the walk and making dinner – after all that, you can settle down for a well-earned rest.

When to get professional help

WHEN YOU HAVE DONE your best to unclutter your space and the clutter seems magically to reappear, or if a particular space in your home or office makes you feel uneasy, it may be time to get professional help.

Certain buildings are affected by an inordinately strong yin or yang energy because of their proximity to certain man-made or naturally occurring phenomena. A space near these buildups of energy can suffer from unpredictable flows of energy. Certain feng shui cures can be used to correct the situation, but you may need an expert to help you work out what is the cause of your clutter. You may particularly need professional help if you live or work near:

* A church
* A cemetery
* A school
* A railway station
* An airport
* Power lines
* A sewerage installation
* An earthquake zone

* A hospital
* A police station
* A college or university campus
* A bus depot
* A highway
* An electricity substation
* A garbage dump
* A site of active volcanoes

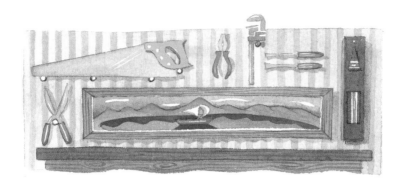

Hospitals, churches, cemeteries, and other areas where great distress is often felt are thought to emanate an excess of yin energy. Too much yin energy entering a space can make uncluttering a very difficult chore – you may feel that you never have enough energy to make it through the day, let alone adding uncluttering to your routine.

Living near high-energy areas, such as schools and electricity substations, can subject you to an excess of yang energy. Where too much yang energy enters your space, you are likely to experience an inability to focus on the task of uncluttering.

Strong aggressive yang energy can cause headaches, family arguments and disharmony, and poor sleep. You will feel unable to see any uncluttering task through, no matter how small the task is.

On a smaller scale, a group of electrical appliances and a main switchboard have a strong pulse of yang energy and will attract clutter. Feng shui experts generally advise placing a yin colored cloth (possibly black, blue or green) over the appliances to balance the excess of yang energy.

Other reasons that clutter can accumulate relates to the position of the building in relation to the surrounding electromagnetic fields. A professional feng shui expert will be able to help alleviate any problems generated by the electromagnetic fields outside your home.

Inside your home, a buildup of electromagnetic radiation generated by your sound system, television, and even your digital bedroom clock radio can attract clutter. To minimize the effect of this electromagnetic radiation, keep your television and sound system inside an "entertainment unit" or special cupboard. If you don't have space for one, drape these pieces of equipment with cloth when they are not in use. Also, keep your digital bedroom clock at least three feet (a meter) away from your head when you are in bed, or get a clock that runs on a battery.

An uncluttering plan

What to do when you get home from work

AS SOON AS YOU walk in the door of your home, take a moment to check your entrance hall. Is it warm and inviting? Is it clear of clothes and paper? Is there a space where you can put the junk mail and letters that are in your hand?

You don't only have to deal with long-term clutter; you must also have a set time to regularly unclutter our home and business space, and an uncluttering system that is uncomplicated and logical.

When considering implementing an uncluttering system, take into account how you interact with your space. Be self-aware about what you do as soon as you enter your home after a day at work, or enter your workplace first thing in the morning. What is your first action? Do you bring the mail in? Is there a stack of newspapers at the entrance to your space? What do you do with the newspapers? What do you do with the mail and junk mail?

The first step is to prevent all unnecessary daily clutter from even coming into your home. First, put a sign on your mail box that reads "No junk mail." Second, near the mail box, have an all-weather paper recycling box large enough to hold any junk mail that still comes through. Unless it is pouring rain and you have no shelter, take the time each day to open your mail and pop any unnecessary information and torn envelopes into the recycling box before you even enter the house.

Once you bring the mail into your home, immediately file it into a series of shallow boxes or trays in the kitchen or family room. Have categories written prominently on the boxes, such as "Bills," "School information," "Bank statements," or "Shopping specials."

If you are bringing in the shopping, have a box set aside in or near the kitchen for any plastic or paper bags that you bring into the house. Keep these bags to a minimum by taking your own shopping bag with you, asking for less packaging, recycling the bags, or returning the bags to retailers who recycle.

You may also use uncluttering as a way of winding down from a day at work. If you have had a frustrating day, you will gain a sense of achievement from having control and making a difference in your own home. Do one small uncluttering task and put a tick beside that task in your "Uncluttering Journal" (see pages 62–63).

When you are uncluttering, keep in mind what you are doing and what you want to create in your home or workplace. Also check your attitude. Clear clutter with thoughts of love, as this will help to generate these feelings within your home. Above all, do not look at clearing as a difficult and tedious chore.

Involving others and making a deal with yourself

IT IS IMPORTANT THAT you involve all family members or work colleagues in the effort to change your surroundings and practices. Clutter is everyone's problem.

In the family, children are often the most difficult to convince that clutter in their bedrooms is not desirable. Clutter can symbolize safety to children, especially if they feel insecure or that the world is changing too quickly or radically for them.

Place or hang a red or pink carnelian over the worst of the clutter. Red carnelian is reputed to dispel lethargy and to help people reconnect with their abilities and gifts; pink carnelian helps re-establish the love between parents and their children.

If you are holding uncluttering meetings that include children, make sure that you keep the uncluttering process and the structure simple enough for the children to understand. Focus on first getting them to place certain items in certain areas. For instance, train them to always put their toys back in their toy box and books back on the shelf. However, make sure that the books actually fit onto the bookshelf and their toys fit into the toy box.

To enforce this new behavior, use a reward system. Build up to more challenging tasks, still keeping the tasks simple. You may use a reward system for yourself too, to help you stay motivated to clear the clutter on a daily or weekly basis. Take some time to visualize exactly how you want your house to look. Cut out pictures of various interiors that you admire and would like to emulate from magazines you are going to throw out. Keep these images in a pretty box and place them by the front door as a reminder of your desire.

Follow each uncluttering session with a treat. Allow yourself to take a break, making sure that your period of rest is as long as the time you spent uncluttering a particular area or space. Do something nurturing during this time, such as having a warm, scented bath or a cup of tea with a good quality piece of chocolate.

Use uncluttering as a way of distracting yourself if you are feeling restless, bored or unable to focus. Also consider doing your uncluttering when you are expecting an important call or email. You will be distracted momentarily from feelings of anxiety, replacing them with a sense of achievement.

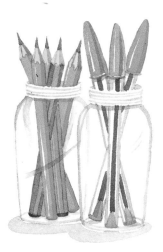

The art of grouping the same things together

WHEN YOU HAVE CLEARED your long-term clutter and have implemented some systems of dealing with daily clutter, your next task will focus on how to store and use the objects you have chosen to keep.

For qi energy to flow among your possessions, you must not only have the surfaces of your interior clean, tidy and populated only with objects that are functional or beautiful and of good quality; you must also make certain that the hidden areas of your space are functional.

Desk drawers and kitchen pantries are some of the worst clutter culprits. You will be amazed how much money you will save by grouping the same things together, and you will also realize how much stuff you have actually stockpiled without knowing it.

Try some of the following suggestions for these problem areas. In both Western and Eastern philosophies, attention to detail is seen as the key to achieving all the important projects in life and work.

DESK DRAWERS

Designate a specific purpose for each drawer – one for letters, stamps, envelopes, address books, and postcode or zip code booklets, another for pens, pencils, erasers, staples, and adhesive tape.

Within each drawer, get separate containers to hold things like rubber bands, paper clips, erasers, and eraser refills.

Arrange the containers so that you can see at a glance what you have. This may indicate that some supplies are needed immediately or in the near future, and will help you control your stock or stationery more effectively.

Also arrange the containers so that there is balance and symmetry in your drawer space, so that qi energy will flow beneficially, particularly for certain aspirations (see pages 14–15).

Certain spaces underneath your desk correspond to the same aspirations as your home or workplace. Subdivide your desk in the same way.

Your drawers will usually be placed under either the "Wealth/Background Information/Inner Wisdom" line or the "Relationships/New Projects/Help from people" line. By clearing your drawers, these aspirations will greatly benefit.

PANTRIES

Sort out your cans and packaged foods. Throw away everything that is past its expiration date.

Group together the cans and packages. You may be surprised to find that you have a large number of the same products.

Purchase clear plastic containers/boxes and store your foodstuffs in categories that suit your usual food choices. For example, have boxes for baking products, condiments and herbs, instant meal kits or specialist gourmet foods that require a distinctive range of ingredients, such as Thai (coconut milk, tom yum paste, kaffir lime leaves, dried mushrooms), Indian (ghee, basmati rice, curry paste, mustard seeds) or macrobiotic food (nori sheets, umeboshi plum paste, buckwheat, brown rice vinegar).

Make a shopping list of things that are missing in your pantry that would help you have quick access to a particular type of meal.

Make an "anti-shopping" list of all the cans and packages that you do not need to buy until you finish off what you have stockpiled.

Checking your progress with photographs

CLEAR PHOTOGRAPHIC EVIDENCE OF the clutter around you is an excellent way to convince yourself and others in your family or business that a problem exists. Further, taking pictures of your space, both the cluttered and uncluttered areas, will provide a benchmark for what needs to be done in each area. Taking photographs of an area at regular intervals gives you tangible evidence that your uncluttering is making a difference.

Buy a good quality photo album specifically for storing photographs of your premise's interior. If you are doing the same exercise for your home and your workplace, buy a photo album for each building. If you have a digital camera, set up folders on your computer to store the photos for each room and area in your space.

If you are using a photo album, divide it into sections, one for each room or area in your home or workplace. Include sections for rooms and areas that are not at the moment suffering from clutter.

1. When you are ready, on a quiet day, take your camera and a notebook and walk to the front door or entrance. From your door or entrance, look outside and take a photograph of your immediate vicinity. Check for poison arrows created by flag or telegraph poles, sharply angled rooflines and straight roads leading to your door (see pages 16–17).

2. Turn back and view your entrance. Jot down your first impressions. Does the area look inviting? Are there boxes and clutter in the area? Can you see clutter in other areas from here? Take a photograph of the whole area, if possible, and then a photograph of each smaller area of clutter.

3. Move through your home and business space as you feel qi energy would move through your space. Qi travels in curved lines. See where you are led. Be especially watchful of clutter that accumulates at the end of a long corridor. Take a photograph of the clutter in this area and make a note in your journal or notebook – you will need to implement a "feng shui cure" before starting to unclutter this area (see pages 16–17).

3. Continue walking through your space and photographing the clutter. In certain areas, the clutter may be hidden, but still causing underlying problems in your life. Be thorough, and take photographs of the interior of all cupboards and drawers. After getting the photographs developed, sort them into the categories you have organized in your photo album or computer. Leave room to put in more photographs, when you have finished uncluttering.

Bring these photos to the first meeting that you and your family or staff have about how to unclutter your shared space (see pages 44–47) – they will inspire, motivate, and help you form action plans to clear the clutter from the targeted areas. Include in your meeting an agreement to assess the uncluttering process photographically at certain regular intervals, such as every two weeks or once a month. Consider setting up a reward system for when particular areas show substantial improvement.

Starting an "Uncluttering Journal"

WHEN YOU ARE SERIOUS about uncluttering your space, an "Uncluttering Journal" is an absolute must. It will help you keep track of the stage at which your uncluttering is. This is especially helpful if you have a family or staff team working with you on the uncluttering process.

The journal can house a multitude of information and ideas. You do not have to use a "day-by-day" planner; any lined journal will do. Choose a book that has good quality paper, as you may want to paste in lists and photographs, as well as write down your impressions of how the project is going and jot down ideas from friends and books (such as this one) that you can implement.

The journal also acts as a symbol of what you are trying to do in your life – simplify and consolidate your lifestyle or business practices. By placing the information on this important topic in one easily accessible book, you are creating a focus for the project and adding depth to the process.

Keep a pen always at the ready near the journal so that any idea can be quickly written down. If you are using a spiral-bound book, keep a pen inside the spirals, so that it is always handy. Consider using the journal for one or all of the following purposes:

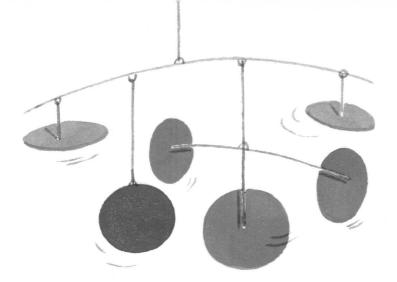

Noting when a 12-month period is up for items that have been stored because you are unsure whether or not you will need them. This date will mark the point when you will need to throw or give away these items if they haven't been used within the 12 months.

Noting a list of stored boxes and where they are stored.

Noting where the clutter is accumulating and what needs to be done to block any poison arrows aimed at the area.

Noting whether the level of clutter has lessened once a wind chime, crystal, or other feng shui cure has been hung over the cluttered area.

Noting whether the level of clutter has lessened by dint of effort, and what systems have been successful in keeping the clutter from piling up again.

Pasting in pictures cut from store catalogues of storage systems or containers that appeal or would suit a specific area in your space.

Noting the list of uncluttering jobs, leaving room beside each entry to tick off what has been done and when the job was completed.

Pasting in photographic evidence and leaving room for further photographs documenting how the space looks after various uncluttering tasks have been completed.

Noting any odd incidents or coincidences after you have uncluttered a space, such as unexpectedly winning a holiday or getting a coveted contract.

Personal clutter

Coping with clutter close to you

CLUTTER AROUND YOU CAN sometimes indicate that you have not wished to focus on yourself or your direction in life. However, it is worth trying to remove the clutter around you – you have many excellent qualities, and the clues to your life's purpose are embedded in the clutter.

One of the most important issues to look into is your sense of identity. You can start doing this by clearing the personal clutter from around you. Where do you find personal clutter? This kind of clutter tends to congregate in the bedroom and bathroom areas, with dressing tables and drawers, wardrobes, the space under your bed, medicine cabinets and bathroom cupboards being the main culprits.

To work out what kind of person you are, before clearing and analyzing the clutter, sit down and make a list of what you think you like and don't like. If this feels too confronting, try making a list for a hero or heroine of a story, and imbue him or her with all your likes and dislikes in terms of clothing styles, colors, shoes, socks and stockings, perfume or after shave, jewelry and accessories. For hints on uncluttering your clothes, shoes, handbags, purses or wallets, see pages 66–69.

We often have things that were given to us by friends and relatives, and that give an indication of how they view us. Sometimes these objects are well off the mark when compared with how we perceive ourselves. If there are items that do not suit your self-image, consider throwing or giving away these items, unless the item was palpably given with love and care. For gift-giving ideas in an uncluttering context, see pages 70–71.

When shopping for personal items, take your list with you and see if your intended purchase enhances your look, lifestyle, or life purpose. If you feel that you just have to have the item, regardless of its not fitting into any of these lists, you may be using "retail therapy" to try to alleviate feelings of stress or emotional upset.

Remember, buying something that you can't truly integrate into your life will only have a very short-term effect on your feelings. Consider saving the money and using it to get something that will nurture you, such as a soothing massage, a weekend away, an evening at the movies, or a meal at your favorite restaurant.

Feng shui uncluttering anecdote

Uncluttering may help you find a partner, either in business or in a personal relationship, once you have made space for that person to come into your life or business. Sandra had been single for some time, and had decided to use feng shui to help her find a mate. She was advised by Rosemary to clear out her bedroom and bathroom. Sandra cleared clothing from her wardrobe and left it half-empty, and her bathroom was treated in the same way. By doing this, she made room for someone to enter her life. Several weeks later she met a man and they have been together ever since.

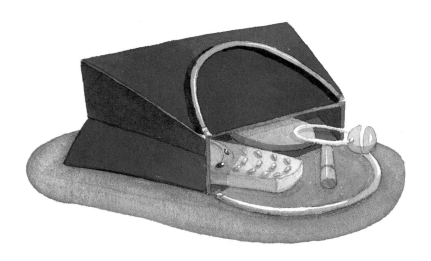

Purses, wallets, and handbags

THE STATE OF YOUR purse or wallet is an indication of the state of your wealth, and of your ability to manifest wealth in your life. An overstuffed wallet full of receipts relating to money long gone and credit cards which have left you in some financial distress is an indication that you do not feel able to move forward in gaining wealth.

When you next have to wait somewhere for a while, such as in a doctor's waiting room or a dentist's office, instead of reading a magazine, clean out your purse and wallet. Arrange your money in order of denomination – this way you will know at a glance how much you really have. Sort through all your credit cards, discount cards and store cards, and decide which ones you really need to carry.

In feng shui, the wealth aspiration corresponds to the elements of wood and water. If you are at home, take your purse or wallet and clear everything out of it – money, cards, written paper scraps, receipts, business cards – everything.

Do not sort anything at this stage. Take a damp cloth and wipe all the lint and dust out of the purse or wallet and burn a stick of incense so that you are activating new energy to enter the purse or wallet (as well as your own financial matters) and clearing out the stagnant energy.

You may want to place a small picture of a tranquil water scene, for instance, or a picture of a beautifully appointed beachside resort with clear blue skies and palm trees in your purse or wallet, indicating an intention to retire early and prosperously. Do not choose pictures of storms, or atmospheric but gloomy seascapes, or sunsets over the water – these pictures will not enhance prosperous energy.

For those who have handbags, the contents can be an easy indication of the state of your life. If your bag is overflowing with stuff, representing the many things you tend to do in a day, uncluttering your handbag and working out what you do and don't need will lead to a similar uncluttering in your life.

If you have too many handbags, consider throwing or giving away those that cannot be matched to your shoes (depending on the fashion) and your clothes.

Feng shui uncluttering tip

If you work at home or if you have a secure office, consider placing your uncluttered purse or wallet in the wealth sector of your desk (see pages 58–59). Or simply place a feng shui coin in your uncluttered purse or wallet to generate a flow of good luck to that part of your life.

Shoes and clothing

SOMETIMES WHEN WE ARE feeling down, buying a nice pair or shoes or a beautiful dress can make us feel much better. However, if the dress or shoes do not suit the rest of our wardrobe, the feeling of pleasure does not remain for long, and soon we need another "fix" to feel happy. This short-term stress solution can lead to long-term financial problems.

Knowing what clothing and shoes suit you and being realistic about your body size and shape will help you unclutter your life. You may also decide to start a personal uncluttering journal in which you can paste all the pictures of clothing, makeup products and tips, fabric, jewelry and other items that you like or feel are suitable for you. This will also help you clear the clutter of magazines that you may have been loath to throw out because there was a picture of an outfit you liked, or a makeup tip you thought was useful. The journal will allow you to clear your room of unnecessary magazines while helping work out what you really like.

To clear your clothing clutter, take out all your clothes and dump them onto your bed or a surface where you can easily sort through them. Assess whether the clothes are in good condition. Those that are in poor condition or are of poor quality should be thrown on a pile marked for immediate disposal or even recycling as cleaning rags.

Next, sort through the clothes that fit you at your current weight and shape. We all have skinny, medium and fat clothes. We sometimes hang onto clothes that symbolize when we were much thinner, theoretically providing us with a path to go back to those days. What this piece of clothing is really doing, however, is stagnating the energy around our self-image and making us feel uncomfortable about where we are now.

Remember that a piece of clothing will usually not, by itself, inspire you to lose weight or become fitter. Owning up to the shape you have now puts you a step closer to doing something about it, if you really feel uncomfortable about how you look. If these wrong-size pieces of clothing are in good condition, put them in a pile marked for your favorite charitable organization. It's often a good idea to sort all your clothes into groups – suits, shirts, trousers, skirts, track pants, sports clothes, coats, and jackets – to help you recognize the clothes you don't wear often. Often the reason that you do not wear a garment is that you have nothing that complements it.

To unclutter your collection of shoes, the first step is to throw out those shoes that are dated, scuffed, the wrong size, or that blister your feet. The second step is to collect the shoes that you feel uncomfortable in or that do not match any of your outfits. Put them in a box and consider having a party at which you can offer your friends their choice of the shoes and clothes you no longer need or want.

Feng shui uncluttering anecdote

Diane had a wardrobe full of clothes and many pairs of shoes, but still felt that she didn't have a thing to wear. In despair, she consulted a professional image consultant to work out, from Diane's skin tone, what colors would suit her. The consultant also helped Diane work out what styles would suit her body shape and frame and make her look slimmer. She threw or gave away all the clothes and shoes that did not suit her, and she found shopping a much easier and less expensive exercise, as she now knew what colors and styles flattered her. This made her feel good and in control.

Giving gifts

GIFTS ARE AN IMPORTANT expression of regard and respect for the person receiving them. However, there are situations in which friends and relatives feel constrained or overly stressed about buying a gift, and sometimes little care or time is taken to select the most appropriate expression of their feelings for you.

Gift giving is an art, and it doesn't always work out right – many of us have a cupboard full of objects that we would rather not have. However, we cherish the thought that our friends and relatives sought to convey.

One way of dealing with this conflict between an unsuitable gift and the genuine expression of love or friendship it represents is to have a special box that will hold your favorite cards, as well as a photograph of the items that various people have given you that have been unsuitable but well meant. This leaves you clear to give or throw the gift away without throwing away the love and affection.

To avoid future gift-giving disasters, consider sending out short gift lists to whoever asks. When giving a present to a friend or relative, do not be afraid to ask for a gift or wish list – coordinate with other friends or relatives to make sure no one is doubling up.

Also, when you are with your friend or relative , if they mention that they wish they had something or want a particular item, make a note of it as soon as you can in your journal or notebook. Have a page set out for each friend and relative that you usually give presents to and jot the ideas on the person's page.

Get family members to pool their money and purchase one large functional or good quality gift instead of giving a number of small, unusable items. Establish ground rules with your family and friends about alternative gift ideas – this may help alleviate the levels of clutter in your home.

There are many thoughtful ways to share your love, regard or respect for another person. You could make a gift bag for a friend into which, every year, you pop a small expression – a beautiful collection of stones, shells, or feathers, for example – of your regard for that friend. Another non-cluttering solution is to take your friend or relative out for a restaurant meal, or cook them a meal at home. You could give them a box of home-baked cookies, a bunch of home-grown flowers or a terra-cotta pot planted with a small "garden" of flowering bulbs. Your resourcefulness and the thought and care you put into simple expressions of your regard will be greatly appreciated.

Household and office clutter

Coping with common household clutter:
some dos and don'ts

VITAL ENERGY COMES INTO your home or business space primarily through the front door or front entrance from the street. Keep this area well aired and free from clutter. Do not store broken items or parts of larger objects in this area – they will block beneficial qi energy from freely entering your space. Also, do not keep shoes around the front door. If you must leave them there, purchase a box in which to put them.

Clutter generated by your children is another important area for which you should consider devising an appropriate system. Place all their papers and homework in one area, but first ask your children where they would like to put their homework and what type of container they require. If your children are allowed to choose how they want to store their paperwork, there will usually be a higher level of compliance and a lower level of clutter – they have become part of the decision-making process, contributing significantly to the clutter solution. Continue to keep them involved in routine clutter sessions, and in re-evaluating your family's organizational systems.

Paper clutter is one of the biggest problems in any family. Where to begin? Start by locating the various bits of paper that make up the clutter. Usually there are piles of paper and magazines in briefcases, on entry tables, kitchen benches and drawers, home offices, desks, garages, sheds, and cars.

Sort these papers into broad categories, such as financial, business and personal. Then take one pile, say "personal papers," and sort it into subcategories, such as evening courses, local events, and cinema or theater listings. Be sure to file only the most current information on events and classes, and to review this subcategory regularly.

If you have a home office, make sure that you can have a separate room for your office and that the paper it attracts and generates is kept separate from the household paper clutter. Develop strategies and timetables to ensure a balance between work and home life, and make time for regular uncluttering in both home and office areas.

If you don't have time to read the daily paper, think about whether or not you need to buy it every day. Perhaps purchase a newspaper only on the days when you will have time to read it. Virtually every newspaper has a website that can give thumbnail sketches of the main stories of the day, so you could incorporate a quick Internet newspaper session each day. If you do buy newspapers, make sure that they are discarded as soon as they have been read (cut out any articles you need to keep first) – they are a fire hazard and can be an emotional drain.

When you have finished uncluttering the various areas in your home and office, light a candle in that area and do something celebratory, such as having a house clearing party. If clutter starts to appear again, check for any hidden poison arrow (see pages 10–11, 16–17) or seek professional feng shui advice (see pages 52–53).

Feng shui uncluttering tip

When out shopping for household items, do not be tempted to buy things just because they are on sale. Take the time to research prices, compare features and shop around for the best deals. When purchasing dinner sets and other dishes, stick to the one pattern and a plain color or design that will match the pattern and can be used more for everyday ware.
Do not stray from this selection, and ensure that you will be able to buy replacement pieces.

Coping with office clutter: the paper chase

WITH THE ADVENT OF computers in modern day business, it was thought that paperless business practices would soon evolve. Strangely enough, this did not happen, and we seem to have as much paper now as we did before.

When you are planning the uncluttering of your office, you will need to use certain strategies, such as regularly going through your files and assessing the items in them in terms of currency, and whether or not you need to keep them to comply with any legal requirements or because of certain industry practices. You will also need to determine whether or not they can – or should – be stored in an off-site facility, or how they can be stored on-site in such a way as to be accessible and easy to update.

However, before you start sorting your papers, you need to have things to store them in, such as expanding files with labels, hanging file folders and their metal frames, and filing cabinets. Before filing, refiling or consolidating your documents, work out a strategy for screening information, and decide on a consistent method of working out where to file the paper. Do not have a "Sort Later" pile – this file is notorious for growing bigger and bigger until it becomes unmanageable. File immediately.

Feng shui uncluttering tip

Is work slow or are there no new contracts coming in? The answer to this dilemma is to clear your desk whenever you finish work, and, in particular, to leave the central area free of any clutter. By doing this, you are symbolically setting up an empty space so that new work can come your way.

Business files can be organized by subject matter, and the material inside your files can be arranged in either alphabetical, geographic or date order. There are many types of business file categories, such as:

* Central files and work files (the latter are the files necessary for the day-to-day running of your business)
* Staff files, including job descriptions, and employees' contact details, resumes, certificates, diplomas and related credentials, professional memberships and societies
* Legal staff requirements, such as general guidelines, safe work practices, policies, and procedures
* Legal business requirements, such as relevant industry practice guidelines and registration documents
* Financial papers, such as bills to be paid, bank books and statements, check books and statements, credit card statements, insurance, investments, payment books and tax statements
* Job manuals and information
* Trade literature, design guides, tender information
* Professional and work-related information, journals and articles
* Competitors' details and information
* Information about forthcoming trade fairs, conferences and seminars.

With all your information filed appropriately and easy to retrieve, you will save valuable time and therefore increase your productivity. Another way of keeping clutter at bay is by keeping your desk clear of paper, using a tray system to keep track of your personal workload. A tray system can be as simple or as complex as is required. It needs to be placed at the first port of call in any business and should be easily accessible – within arm's reach. Simple "In" and "Out" trays can be established.

Consider having a "Pending" tray for work that has to be completed within one or two days. Also include a tray for weekly and monthly tasks, as well as for "Reading," "Filing," and "Receipts."

Books and magazines

IT IS ALSO WORTHWHILE to look at how you deal with the clutter of books and magazines. If your work is based on gathering and using information, before you throw anything away, you will need to check whether your books, magazines, and other sources of information are current and still creditable.

It is important to keep books and magazines that are necessary for your work in one place, so that you do not waste time searching for information in various parts of your home or business space.

The first step to uncluttering the books and magazines in your home is to gather them all into one area, if you can – it is not always possible. If you have a great number of books and magazines, try creating an area that is substantially devoted to their storage.

The next step is to sort them by subject matter or by magazine name (and date). You may find that you have an inordinate number of cookbooks. The question to ask yourself is: "How many cookbooks do I need to cook a meal?" Consider keeping only those cookbooks that fit into your current lifestyle, taste and budget. Donate the remainder to your local library or your favorite charitable organization. You may also wish to transcribe or photocopy your favorite recipes and place them in a binder.

Reference materials, such as encyclopedias, usually need to be kept up-to-date. Ask yourself whether you really need a complete set of encyclopedias that came out in 1960. There are now available a number of excellent encyclopedias online and on CD-ROM – these take up very little space on your bookshelf or desk. Do not forget that you can always donate your reference books to your local library, where you can go see them whenever you want.

You will need to decide whether to keep or throw out your magazines. Your stash of magazines may go back many years, and you may have forgotten why you chose to keep individual issues. Look at whether or not you are keeping a particular issue just for one article. If you are, simply photocopy the item and place it in a plastic insert or sleeve in a folder.

Consider donating the intact magazines to your local library or your doctor's waiting room. Review your folder yearly to see which articles – if any – you have used during that time, then decide which should be kept and which should be thrown out. Photographic magazines are often hard to let go because of their array of usually exceptional quality pictures. Your best solution would be again to give them to your local library or school, where they will be appreciated and used and where you can still access them whenever you want.

Feng shui uncluttering anecdote

Susan collected all her old magazines, product catalogs and articles and used them to create a picture calendar for a preschool child. She cut out all the pictures and arranged them in groupings and gave each day a different theme. The child to whom she gave it enjoyed looking at the pictures and identifying the subjects. As well as being a functional calendar and a delightful gift, it also became a pictorial learning tool.

Uncluttering the bathroom and kitchen

THE BATHROOM AND KITCHEN are among the most neglected yet overused rooms in the house. These two areas have an unnerving capacity for clutter. Here are a few tips on how to cope with the clutter caused by leftover medicines and cleaning products.

In the bathroom, clutter usually accumulates in the medicine cabinet and in the cupboards under the bathroom sink. The main clutter culprits are leftover medicines, potions and creams that we have saved "just in case" we need them. It is more than likely that all these leftover products will have passed their expiration date before we use them again. Discard these items immediately.

Beauty products and half-used specialty soaps are other bathroom clutter culprits. Ask yourself how many beauty products you really need. Be brave and throw out all the bits of cream that you have stored. Alternatively, use all the cream you have before buying any more. Take note of what beauty products work for you and which you prefer. You may wish only to purchase products that have not been tested on animals, for instance. Purchase only these products and use them right up, to the very last drop.

Sometimes we also manage to accumulate half-used or almost finished specialty soaps – they are made from special nurturing ingredients and essential oils, and have often cost quite a lot of money. One solution is to grate all the remains and roll them into compact soap balls.

Examine your cleaning products for both the bathroom and the kitchen. Consider using only environmentally friendly cleaning products, those that have not been tested on animals and do not contain certain noxious chemicals.

Read the labels to find out whether you have products that have been touted as the right cleaning agent for a particular surface but contain much the same ingredients as any other cleaning product. If so, use them up but don't buy them again – use the cleaning products you already get for other surfaces.

In reality, we only need a few products, and most cleaning agents can double up for many different types of cleaning jobs. Decide what products you wish to keep and which are most effective for your purposes, and stick to those.

A Final Incentive

UNCLUTTERING IS ONE OF the best ways of reorganizing your life. However, the technique is not only about simplifying your possessions. By taking stock of what you have, you will learn some surprising facts about yourself.

Often we do not give ourselves the time or the energy to tune into our thoughts and feelings. However, by following the suggestions in this book and tailoring them to your circumstances, you will find that a whole new world of possibilities and opportunities can emerge for you because you have more insight about yourself.

By knowing yourself, and by focusing on the details of life, you can work out a clear path as to what else you need to do or to be. By simplifying the physical clutter, you will clear the emotional clutter that has been with you since you have been a child and which has stopped you from achieving your dreams.

Let the uncluttering suggestions help you clear and simplify your life and you will never need to feel held back again. Good luck!

This edition published by Barnes & Noble, Inc.,
by arrangement with Lansdowne Publishing

2001 Barnes & Noble Books
Reprinted 2002

ISBN 0-7607-2979-4

M 10 9 8 7 6 5 4 3 2

Commissioned by Deborah Nixon
Production Manager: Sally Stokes
Text: Antonia Beattie and Rosemary Stevens
Illustrator: Sue Ninham
Designer: Avril Makula
Editor: Sarah Shrubb
Project Coordinator: Kate Merrifield

Set in Granjon and Matrix on QuarkXPress
Printed in Singapore by Tien Wah Press (Pte) Ltd